Reb

Stories from T

By

Noelle Blackburn

Table of Contents

If you are reading this book, I am going to assume that you know at least enough about reborns that I do not need to take time to give a detailed explanation of what they are and why they exist. This is a hobby that many people are just discovering, but that some have been pursuing for decades. This book is for anyone interested in Reborns and wanting to know more about them and what they mean to those who have them.

The quest to make ever more lifelike dolls has been in practice for many years, and with new technology, such as 3D printing available, artists are making this happen every day. Doll crafters take their art very seriously and some of the most beautiful examples of reborning have come about in the last few years.

Those of us who collect them and adopt them and love them for their uniqueness and detail also take them very seriously. We are dedicated to caring for them, in varying degrees. Some treat these beautiful dolls as they would a living, breathing baby. Others keep them as collectables and intend to pass them on to relatives as heirlooms. Some find comfort in them after the loss of a child or when they cannot have children. Alzheimer's patients are finding increasing relief in them as it gives them someone to care for and hold near.

As of the writing of this book, the "Reborn Movement" is still expanding throughout the world. There are more people devoted to the care and creation of Reborns in the United States every day, and Britain has already had a large Reborn following for some time. I find the stories of people who love these babies incredibly interesting, as I have a passion for them as well. This book is intended to share the stories of others who feel passionately about Reborn babies with those who feel the same, those who are simply curious and those who are considering adopting a Reborn but have not done so yet.

Whether you are an artist, a parent, a potential parent or a collector, there will likely be something of interest for you in the following stories. I have asked the people who were involved in the creation of this book to tell me their stories honestly. I wanted to include their experiences, both positive and negative with everyone who reads this book. Reborns can be wonderful, but the reactions you get from others can vary widely. Some people fear the 'Uncanny Valley,' and are creeped out by the mere idea of a doll that looks so lifelike. Others think it is okay to be a collector, but take issue with people treating the dolls as real babies. Friends and family members can become weirded out by the affection you show your Reborn, and it can cause strains on relationships.

The other side to the coin, is that these dolls can also calm you, relax you and give you someone to love. They can fill an emotional void and give you a hobby to occupy your time. The stories provided in this book are emotional, personal and included to let others know what Reborns are all about. If you are a Reborn parent looking to feel less alone, these stories may comfort you. If you are considering adopting a Reborn, they may help you to understand more fully what it involves. If you are simply curious about what the draw is to these babies, read more below to find out.

Thank you for reading, and I hope that you find comfort in the stories of others.

2016 Noelle Blackburn

Dave and Kathy

Tahoe, California

The author asked us to choose from a list of questions to answer about or experiences as reborn parents and I thought the most important one on the list, was what made us decide to adopt our first reborn. I think we might be unusual, in the respect that we are not really collectors of much of anything, have not lost a child and chose not to have children together as opposed to having any medical reason why we couldn't. We were just busy being a couple of hard working people and didn't ever feel it was the right time to bring a baby into the world.

I am 53 years old now and my husband, David, is 55. We run a small business out of our home and enjoy spending time outdoors. Our life together has been adventurous, free spirited and for the most part, enjoyable. As we have grown older, I, personally, have considered why we never had any children, why that was never a priority, and feelings of regret occasionally surfaced. I wanted to hold a baby, but with no children and no grandchildren, that was very unlikely to happen. Sometimes it bothered me more than others.

I talked to my husband about these feelings and he agreed, that it frequently crossed his mind and he, too, wondered what life would have been like if we had made the journey into parenthood. Not much came of this session of truth, other than both of us feeling that we understood the other just a little bit better.

It was a couple of months after that when I had my first experience with a reborn. I was part of a women's crafting circle that met every other week. Each of the ladies had a particular interest in some kind of art or craft and we would bring in our pieces to show one another, have a few drinks and a few laughs and ooh and awe at one another's creations. One of the more recent members of the group, a younger gal by the name of Tracy, mentioned that she had been working for a couple of years as a "reborner." None of us ladies had ever heard of such a thing and the poor girl was pretty much immediately overwhelmed by our questions. She happened to have photos of her creations with her on her phone, and none of us believed her when she told us the beautiful babies we were seeing weren't real, but were, in fact, dolls.

We begged her to bring one in for us to see, and at the next meeting, she did. I was floored by how real her work looked. The baby doll had tiny little finger and toenails, tipped with white. The legs and arms had chubby baby wrinkles just like a real baby and the skin had been painted in layers with imperfections, tiny blue veins and the body was weighted so the baby felt real when you held it in your arms. The hair was rooted by hand, thin and wispy like that of a newborn. I fell in love the second he was placed in my arms. That particular baby was already sold, but I approached Tracy after our meeting and begged her to make me one. At that point, cost was not even on my mind, I knew that Dave and I had to have one of these little treasures.

Tracy told me what to expect, it would take her eight to ten weeks to create our little darling. The cost would be five hundred dollars. I chose a boy, put a deposit of 250 dollars down and exchanged information with her. Then, I headed home to tell David what I had done.

He was skeptical at first. He has always been the more financial minded of the two of us, and to be honest, sometimes his practical nature drives me crazy. He is a planner through and through and I...well, I like to just do things at the spur of the moment when they feel right.

"500 dollars for a doll?" he asked, for the second time, looking up at me over the cup of coffee he held in front of him.

"He's more than just a doll," I told him.

His skeptical look did not change. "If it makes you happy," he said.

I didn't push the matter further. I carried on with daily chores. I waited for time to pass, and it did, extremely slowly. David, having not ever seen our future new arrival, was not bothered at all by the wait time, but I was going stir crazy. As the weeks passed by, Tracy contacted me once a week or so to let me know what progress she had made on our baby boy, the little guy that I had decided to name Thomas.

She was a little farther ahead than she thought she would be at the last conversation, and was hoping to be finished with him by the next meeting the following week. I felt my heart begin to beat faster and felt the excitement bubbling up in me. I tried to tell myself that this was silly. I was an adult woman after all, and no matter what, this was really just a doll, albeit an expensive one. I knew I was kidding myself. I remembered the feel of that first baby in my arms and I couldn't wait to have one of my own.

The day before the crafter's circle, I could not settle down. I was like the nervous husband pacing the waiting room when his wife is in delivery. I tried everything to keep myself occupied, but failed every time. I thought of calling Tracy to ensure that she was still bringing him to the meeting, but didn't want to seem like I was pressuring her. I reminded myself that without her, there would be no Thomas in the first place. I had a rough time trying to sleep that night and kept getting up to use the bathroom and look at the clock. The day passed more slowly than I ever recalled a day passing and by the time I was ready to leave for the crafter's circle, I was so excited that I could barely breathe. What if something had gone wrong and she hadn't finished him? What would I do if she didn't have him ready? Surely, she would have called me.

My worries were unfounded. When I pulled up to the restaurant where we held our meetings, Tracy was there, standing by her car. She waited for me to park, and then walked with me to her vehicle. Inside her SUV, strapped into a baby carrier in the back seat, was our little Thomas. He was 20 inches and 4.9 pounds of absolute perfection and I felt tears spring to my eyes when she handed him to me. He had blue eyes, light, sandy-brown hair and was everything I had dreamed of. I hugged Tracy and thanked her, paid her and then stood there, admiring her work and my new baby. I couldn't wait to get home and show David. I had no doubt that his view of my "expensive doll" would change once he saw and held Thomas for himself.

I realized I didn't have a car seat or anything else for a baby, and I also realized how much explaining I would have to do should I get pulled over for anything. The baby looked so real that I was certain he would fool anyone. The meeting held no interest for me that night, and I carefully put Thomas in the back seat of the car, strapping him in with the belt and ensuring he would not roll off the seat should I need to stop fast.

I drove home, wondering what my husband would say when he saw him, and going over a list of things I would need to get for our new baby. I guess you could say at that point, I went from being a married woman with no children, to a mom. It really was that simple. I held him close to me for only a few minutes, in the parking lot of a restaurant and already I knew that he was meant to be mine. He was more than just a doll to me then, and he has grown to be a solid member of our family over the last couple of years.

When I walked in the door at home. Dave was sitting on the couch, half reading a novel and half staring at the television. He looked up and smiled at me. I sat down beside him with Thomas in my arms and my husband looked at me quizzically. "Whose baby is that? Are we sitting?"

I giggled. "This is the baby I told you about. This, is Thomas."

"The *doll*?" he asked, his face of confusion suddenly became one of amazement.

I nodded.

"No wonder it was 500 bucks," he said.

"Would you like to hold him?" I asked.

He looked at me curiously, his eyes flashing back and forth between me and Thomas, then shook his head, firmly. "He's all yours."

I was crushed. Perhaps he didn't get how I felt about it. To me, Thomas would be the baby we had never had. He was more than just a doll, but many of the things I had hoped for and wanted all these years encompassed in a tiny body. I already loved him.

Thinking it was better not to voice my opinions right then, I spent the next few days getting odd looks from David as I clothed, fed and ordered things online for the new baby. He never said anything about it, but I saw his eyebrows raise on more than one occasion. I began to find it funny, in some way. It was like an invisible line had been drawn in the sand between Dave and I. Perhaps he thought that I had lost my mind. Still, I was happier than I had ever been, carrying my little bundle of joy around the house with me. I was still amazed by how realistic he looked and how amazing it felt to have him in my arms.

A few days later, I put Thomas down in his new bassinet for a nap, and decided to go for a shower. I gathered my things, calling down the stairs to Dave that I would be in the shower if he needed me for anything.

After showering and changing into some comfortable clothes for evening, I was toweling my hair dry when I caught sight of something that made me feel warmer inside than even the shower had done. When I walked into the bedroom, David was sitting at the edge of our bed, rocking Thomas back and forth in his arms. He looked guiltily up at me and then smiled. "He looked lonely," he said, by way of explanation.

"You have to admit that he's cute," I said.

Dave looked down at him and then up at me. "I never said he wasn't."

**

Things have been good ever since. In June of this year, we adopted our second reborn, a little girl slightly smaller than Thomas that we named Gracie. She didn't have to wait for daddy to fall in love with her. We take our babies everywhere with us. They ride in car seats, eat with us and go out when we go. Most people just glance our way and make the assumption that they are living, breathing children, and we have only had a few people ask us outright if they are dolls. We readily tell them they are our babies when asked, and don't pay much attention to the few who find it strange. This our life. Our life as a family, and that is good enough for us.

Birmingham, Alabama

My name is Sarah and I am twenty-three years old and live in Alabama. I first got into reborns as a doll collector. I used to focus my collection on porcelain dolls, I started receiving them for my birthday when I was about twelve, and I kept collecting them ever since. A friend of mine bought me my first reborn baby for Christmas four years ago, and I was instantly thrilled with her. She looked so real and was so much more cuddly than a porcelain doll. I loved holding her, and named her Annabeth.

Once Annabeth became part of my life, I started to feel more like a mother and less like a collector. Maybe it was the feel of the baby in my arms, but I just couldn't think of her as a doll. She was too much like a real baby to just be put on a shelf. I was only working part time and things were tight financially, but I found ways, through shopping at local thrift stores and bargain outlets to get her the same kind of a set up that a real baby would have. Each morning I dress her and feed her and rock her. I leave her with my mom when I go to work and pick her up after.

At first, I think my mom was a little weirded out by the idea of a doll being treated like a real baby, but eventually she sat down and talked to me about it. She agreed it was better than having a real baby until I was financially able to support one and emotionally ready. I wasn't even dating anyone then, and even mom had to admit that there was something addictive about holding Annabeth. "She won't outgrow her clothes," she pointed out. She had a point. She also doesn't poop, get sick, or scream in the middle of the night. She's kind of perfect, really.

Some people say that reborn parents are just lazy and don't want to deal with the temper tantrums and so on that really babies have. Not true, in my opinion. Reborn parents choose to care for someone who actually doesn't require it. Is that laziness? Craziness? Whatever your opinion is, this is my hobby and I enjoy it. I love the feel of Annabeth in my arms. I love dressing her and playing with her and feeling like there is someone there I can talk to that is always there to listen.

I'm proud to be the mommy of a reborn baby.

Amy and Mark

San Francisco, California

We adopted our first reborn after a recommendation from our therapist. We'd lost our first child, a little girl, just days after she was born, to a heart condition. We sought therapy to deal with the grief, and the counselor mentioned getting a reborn to help us heal. The idea was not that we try to replace our lost daughter with a doll, but rather that the doll would give us something tangible to hold and a place to point the unfinished words we still wanted to say to our little girl.

Honestly, we were both skeptical at first. Being the type of people who engaged in what one would consider 'normal' activities and not the type who got caught up in flights of fancy, the idea of carrying around a doll, even if it was just at home, seemed like exactly the opposite of what we thought we were about. Some weeks later, when we were even deeper into the grieving process, with no light at the end of the tunnel, I decided to look at reborn babies online. I was amazed at what I found. Many of them did not look like dolls at all. They looked just like real babies, and my heart skipped a beat as I scrolled through a particular doll maker's website. There was a baby who looked so much like our little girl.

I grabbed Mark from the kitchen, and asked him to come look at what I had found. He, too, was amazed. We decided to go ahead and order the one that looked like our little girl. I was nervous pressing the payment button. What if she got here and we were creeped out instead of relieved? What if it made the pain worse to realize we were holding a doll instead of the baby that should have been ours?

Days went by, and when the doll arrived, I had Mark right beside me. We were both curious, perhaps both a little terrified of what we were about to experience. When we opened the box and removed the packing though, all I felt was love. Her tiny little hands and perfect little feet reminded me how much I had loved and still loved our daughter, here with us or in heaven. Her face was so lovely, and when I lifted her from the box and held her against me, I cried like I hadn't been able to since the day we lost our baby.

She allowed us to let go of some of the pent up emotions we held inside. We had both been trying to remain strong for the other, and although it hurt to hold a baby that I knew was not ever going to breathe, grow up, get married, or do any of the things we had envisioned for our child's future, she was also a comfort just to cuddle. When I handed her to Mark, his eyes welled with tears and he snuggled her tiny body into his chest.

We didn't start treating her like a real baby. Instead, we put her in the guest bedroom, snuggled safely into the middle of the queen sized bed. We would go in and hold her together, or alone, and talk to her, read to her. I dressed her in different outfits only occasionally, but it was enough to know that she was there. As time went on and we began to finally see our future forming again, we realized how instrumental in that she had been. She allowed us to feel like our love could go somewhere, like the months of our life we had spent preparing for our daughter had not been wasted.

Even after all this time, I still pick her up and hug her now and again. She reminds me of the child we lost, but she also reminds me that there is always hope for a new beginning, and even in the darkest times, a hug can make things better.

We may not be like some of the other reborn parents out there. We don't take her everywhere and feed her and buy her gifts at holidays, but we love her just the same. She helped us through the worst of times, and for that, she will always have a place in our hearts and homes.

Dana

Carson City, Nevada

When the author asked me to talk about my reborns, I was really excited. I looked at her list of topics and picked one that is close to my heart. "What do other people think of your babies?"

Before becoming a reborn artist myself, I became a mommy to one of my own. I am not desperate for love, nor children. I am happily married and have two natural children of my own, ages eight and eleven, one girl and one boy. I actually got into the reborn movement on accident, finding a doll show and exhibit at a hotel in Las Vegas five years ago. It was then that I saw my first reborn doll and was stunned by the amount of care and detail that went into creating them. As an artist and crafter myself, I became interested in them from a purely professional standpoint. That is, until one of the reborners offered me one to hold.

Is there anything better than holding a newborn baby? Immediately all of the feelings I'd had upon holding my own two babies after birth came back to me. I fell head over heels for these babies. I waited until we got home, and then used the internet to start searching for one of my own. I may never have actually purchased one at such high cost had I not seen them up close for myself. I knew that they took weeks and often months to create, and I knew that they were worth it.

A few weeks later, the reborn I had bought from an artist on Ebay arrived and I unboxed her, anxious to show my kids and get their take on the baby. At first, they were convinced she was real. I had to explain to them that she was a doll, but that we would be careful handling her as if she were a real baby. They both took to her as if she were real, calling her their sister. I wasn't sure if I should discourage the behavior or not, so I let them decide what they wanted to treat her like.

As for my husband, he thought the hobby was 'cute' and encouraged me to enjoy it. "Nothing better than holding a baby," he said. "Especially one that's always in a good mood."

A lot of people probably think I'm crazy. I work from home, full time and also have the two children to care for, and here I am with a doll baby that I care for as well. They have no idea how much I love all my children...including Ashlyn, the reborn. I do take her with me when we go places. I talk to her and dress her. I bathe her and do her hair. My husband has no issue with this, even though he does not express a direct interest in it. The kids want to include her in the things we do as a family, and I let them do it. It makes them happy, and yes, they do realize that she is not a real baby, but it doesn't matter to them. They love her.

Now to address the author's question. What do people think about my reborn? Well, since then, I have adopted another, a little boy that we call Gabe. Honestly, most of the time people don't even seem to notice that they aren't real babies. If I am holding them in public, people just say "awe" as they pass. Sometimes people will ask how old they are, and I just give them a random number. Is this deception? Perhaps. Is that your real hair color? Who cares? I would rather not get into a long and involved conversation where people then question my sanity. I am not ashamed that my babies make me happy. Most of these people I will probably never see again anyway.

The people who are brave enough to ask if the babies are dolls have been a mixed bag of reactions. Some of them are just blown away that a doll could look so real. Others want to know how to find one of their own. Still others, shake their head without saying anything and walk away. I think they must be a little afraid of the babies, or perhaps of me. Oh well. Opinions. Everyone is entitled to them. I've really only had a couple of rude remarks, once when a couple behind me said "Thank God that's a doll, because the woman shouldn't be allowed to raise real children," and once when a pregnant woman got offended that I was buying things at a local Wal-Mart for my reborn. Did she think I was going to buy everything out so there would be nothing left for her child? I wish I had that kind of money.

Otherwise, it has all gone pretty well. My parents live states away and rarely come to visit, as do my husband's parents, but when they have come to visit, they have been not only accepting, but cooed and awed at the babies as if they were real grandchildren. I think it all goes back to that feeling of holding a baby. It does something to warm the soul.

I am not afraid to take the reborns out to the park and play with them with the other children. I love to interact with other families, and thus far, have made some good friends who I wouldn't know otherwise if it hadn't been for their curiosity about the babies.

For the last couple of years I have been designing reborns myself. It is a lot of work, especially since I hand root all of the hairs on their heads and their tiny eye-lashes. It is rewarding work, though. Watching them become ever-more realistic through the different stages thrills me, and seeing the completed baby makes me proud of the craft I have chosen to involve myself with.

I do not sell my dolls, but rather donate them where they are needed the most. I have donated a handful of them to hospitals where they are given to elderly dementia patients, and about as many to hospitals, to be given out to grieving parents after the loss of a child. I like to tell myself that these babies make people as happy as my own have made me, and that they are serving the purpose I intended for them as I painstakingly created them.

The honest truth, is that I really don't care what people think about me, my family or those who think it is weird. I love all of my babies. I will most likely always be devoted to these gorgeous dolls. They mean a lot to me on a lot of different levels and I am proud to have them, to create them and to donate them to enrich the lives of others.

I hope that if you are reading this and have experienced some of the weirdness of other people regarding your own reborns, that you realize their opinions don't matter. Do what makes you feel is right.

New Orleans, Louisiana

Am I crazy? I live in New Orleans. We're all a bit crazy here, or so the tourists say. I am a reborn collector as well as parent. I currently have over fifty dolls and don't intend to stop. When I die someday I will leave them all to my kids.

Reborn dolls became a part of my life when a friend of mine starting making them. I really didn't like them when I first saw them. That was back before the techniques had advanced to the stage they have in recent times and I thought the babies were a bit...ugly. Still, she could make dolls custom to the wishes of the clients, so I ordered one, a boy, to look like my first born, Brandon. She did a good job with him, and even though he wasn't a perfect replica of my oldest boy, he was close enough to make me smile. I set him in the corner of my bedroom on a dresser, and often looked at him, admiring the craftsmanship put into him. One day I was cleaning the room, and picked him up for a cuddle. I don't know exactly what it was, but after having had him for months, holding him close that day felt different. It was as if I were really holding my son again, right after he was born. I was flooded with a peaceful and warm feeling and stood there, gently rocking him.

From that day on, my interest in reborns grew. Since then I have amassed quite a collection of these little babies. Some of them have their eyes open, some of them are asleep. Some of them are preemies and some of them are babies and some of them are toddlers. I'm sure that there are people out there that would not understand why I collect them, but truthfully, seeing them just makes me happy. I know that they are always in the mood for a hug. They are always waiting for me when I get home, and they never grow up and move away or get sick. It is nice to know that you can love someone unconditionally without worrying about the things we worry about every day with human friends and relatives.

I have a room in my small house devoted to them, that I have dubbed "the nursery," and that is where I keep the majority of my babies. I don't take them out in public, I don't treat them exactly as one would a real child, but I go in at night and read to them and give them hugs and kisses. There really are no favorites. I love them all for different reasons. My first reborn still has a special place in my heart though, and in the nursery. I keep him in the center of the crib I bought for them, resting happily amongst his brothers and sisters.

Why do I think reborns are becoming so popular? For a lot of reasons, really. They fulfil a need within us to give love. I think for some people, they are the ultimate collectible quest. Trying to find the perfect baby that looks more and more realistic becomes an obsession. I don't see how this could be a bad thing, unless you are spending money that you don't have to spend or neglecting other things or people in your life because of it. I think most people who start buying reborns just like looking at them and enjoy the way they mimic a real baby. I can't speak for everyone else, but I can definitely say that for me, they are a comfort. I feel less alone surrounded by my babies, and I like knowing they are there.

I intend to keep collecting them and loving them.

Kelly

Portland, Oregon

I don't collect or have any reborn dolls myself, but I chose to include my story in this book to talk about the experience I have with a reborn doll. My sister is autistic, and aged 17. She has always struggled to show affection with others, and has a lot of quirks when it comes to being out in unfamiliar places. She likes her routines and doesn't appreciate interruptions in them. She has attended special classes for a number of years, and goes through phases where she does okay for a while and then those times when she seems to close off the rest of the word and not do so well, even with familiar instructors.

Last Christmas, my step-dad got her a reborn doll. At that point, my sister was not interested in trying to care for herself at all. Everything was a struggle. Eating, bathing, dressing, all of it. She had always shown an interest in pretty dolls, the china ones and others that came with ruffled dresses and accessories. And after getting her reborn doll, we noticed changes in her.

She cared for the doll as if it were a real baby, or at least to the extent that she was able to understand the needs of a real baby. She is very intelligent, she just has trouble associating things as most of us would. We bought her some outfits for the baby, some diapers and bows for her hair. Soon, we found that my sister was doing things alongside the reborn, like taking care of her own hair, eating and even trying to converse with her.

She carries the baby around with her, always treating it with reverence and carefully cuddling it to her. She shows the reborn real affection, love and tenderness. Some might find that weird, but for us, it is a step in the right direction. To see her happy and smiling, to see her care for herself and something else, has been amazing. I firmly believe that these dolls are useful in therapy. Perhaps they can reach a level with some people that another person can't. They don't judge, they don't struggle and they are able to be molded into what you want them to be. All I know, is that for my sister this has made a huge difference in her life, and in ours.

Paisley and Brian

Long Island, New York

My fascination with reborns started when I was seventeen. I saw one on the TV and knew right away that I had to have one of my own. I couldn't believe how lifelike they looked. I have always suffered with anxiety attacks, and wondered to myself if having a baby to cuddle and look after would help me to relax. It did exactly that. Since my first reborn, Chelsea, arrived, I have adopted one more, a boy named Xavier. I am now 26, and have been devoted to my love of reborns since the day Chelsea showed up in my life.

When I began taking care of her and considering myself a reborn mom, I was single. I didn't think too much about how other people would react to my baby. About a year after getting Chelsea, I met Brian and we began dating more often and more seriously over the next few months. I was worried how he would react when he saw that I wasn't just a collector, but that I treated my reborn baby as if she were real. The first time I introduced them, I think he was a little uncomfortable, not sure how to react, but after spending time with us, he seemed to accept it with no issue. He asked me some questions about why I did what I did, and I was honest with him. I told him about the former anxiety attacks and that loving her gave me something else to focus on.

Brian is now as involved in the lives of the reborns as I am, and proudly calls them his children. We have not ruled out the possibility of having natural children someday, but for now, these babies are enough for us until we feel that we are ready to move forward with a pregnancy. I think of it as experience for the real thing. At least we will know how to change a diaper!

Kayla

Dallas, Texas

I'm happy to tell the story of my daily routine with Max, my reborn. Max is 20" long, weighs 5 lbs. 4 oz. and is the love of my life...so far anyway. I got him as a gift from a friend when I graduated high school three years ago, and my life has changed for the positive since he came into it. I treat him as a real baby in every way that I can, including diapering, feeding and buying him gifts for his birthday and holidays. I love him just as if I had given birth to him and really have no desire to listen to the detractors. He's my baby and that's all there is to it.

Our daily routine:

I wake up in the morning and brush my teeth, use the bathroom and get dressed, and then immediately pick up Max from the bassinet he sleeps in beside my bed. I give him a diaper change, using baby wipes gently—he has a cloth body. I then powder him just a little, with baby powder, and put on a fresh diaper. I don't change him too many times per day, but usually at least twice.

From there I change him from his jammies he wore the night before into a fresh, clean outfit for the day. He has lots of clothes, and I often take him out shopping with me to buy new things. Just as parents do with their children, I find him special things that I think he would like and add them to my normal shopping list.

Once I have max dressed, I make him a bottle of formula and carry him to the living room, where I put on cartoons for him and feed him his bottle. The type of bottle I use is a slow flow nipple attached to a nurser bag bottle. I keep a rag around to catch any dribbles. When he finishes his bottle, I put him in a baby bouncer and let him watch his cartoons for an hour or so.

Then we do some tummy time for a half an hour or so, and I read him to sleep. When he gets up in the afternoon, I give him baby cereal or bananas for lunch and we usually go out for a walk. I have a stroller for him that has a net over it to keep the bugs away and offer him some shade. It gets really hot in Texas, and the sun is unforgiving, so I try to keep him shaded as much as possible so he will not fade. I walk him through the park and we often stop to feed the ducks and geese any leftover bread we have.

I get lots of questions about him, how old he is, etc. Most people do not realize that he is not a real baby. I never tell them unless they ask me directly, but most people don't. He looks real enough, especially under the netting that it doesn't come up often. I don't intentionally fool people. I'm not seeking attention. All I want is a quiet walk with my baby boy in the park, but I also don't see a reason to create drama where there isn't any. So when people ask a simple question, like, how old? I just say two months and keep walking. It works to keep curiosity at bay. I figure people walk their dogs in strollers, this shouldn't be that strange.

When we get home, I make something for dinner while Max plays in his bouncer or jumper with his toys. I like to give him rattles and soft cuddly blankets to snuggle with. I do realize that he has no ability to truly play with them, but as props, they make him seem even more real to me and I like that.

He usually has a bottle and then some kind of oatmeal and fruit combination for dinner, and then it is bath time. I have a bath chair for him, made out of mesh, and I use a bowl of lavender scented water and a rag to gently clean him up. I only wash his hair (mohair) occasionally and brush it out with a soft-bristled baby brush. When I do wash it, I use a baby detangling wash to make it easier to brush.

When his bath is done, I wrap him in a hooded baby towel and dry him off, snuggling with him and singing to him softly as I get him into another clean diaper and his chosen outfit for bed. Most of the time he gets dressed in the little baby pajamas with feet.

After that. I rock him to sleep. Of course, there are plenty of times that our routine doesn't go like that. Responsibilities and work and life in general throw things off, but we stick to that schedule whenever possible. I try to take him everywhere with me that I can.

My mom and dad are both supportive of me, although it did take them a little while to get used to the idea of having a reborn as a grandchild. I think they see how happy Max makes me and that makes them happy, so they have decided to accept it at face value.

I don't worry a lot about what people think about my love for Max. Either they accept it, or they don't. Either way I will still take care of him as my son. He makes me happy and gives me purpose, and that's all anyone is really looking for, I think.

Sheila, age 32

Boston, Massachusetts

I can't have children of my own. It's a fact that I have struggled to accept for a number of years, and although I wish there were something that could be done about it, there isn't. I found reborns when I was in a forum with other women discussing their inability to have babies, and someone suggested that these dolls offer comfort to people like me. In the beginning, I thought they were suffering from some serious mental illness. I was way too old to be playing with dolls.

It wasn't until I saw a couple of photos in that same chat room and couldn't tell that they weren't real babies that my interest became piqued. How could any doll look so real? I did some external research, reading about the popularity of reborns in Europe and what they were used for. It seemed a lot of people used reborns in a therapeutic way. Some couples used them to assist in the grieving process, and some used them to help them deal with the empty feeling caused by a lack of children. There were also the people who simply collected them because they thought they were fun and the ones who created them and sold them. I wondered at that point if it was really so crazy after all.

I looked into different artists and the many types of reborns that were available before really narrowing down what I thought I might be interested in. I decided that if I was going to go in, I might as we go all in, and got a set of twins, one boy and one girl, that I named Michael and Makayla. When they arrived, the feeling of opening that box was like no other. I was nervous, excited, a little terrified even. When I held them in my arms, I imagine that it must have been a similar feeling to what a parent feels after the delivery of their child. I felt like my babies had finally come home. They were so perfectly weighted, and fit so nicely into the crook of my arm, that it was hard to remember that they weren't real.

I found a part of myself that was missing. I do know that they are not real in the actual sense of the word. I am completely aware that they aren't made of flesh and bone, but they fill a spot in me that nothing else could, so what they are made out of is really irrelevant.

Am I trying to replace the babies I can't have with dolls?

Maybe. Is that so bad? My reborns make me happy. Isn't that all that really matters at the end of the day for everyone?

Leah, age 34

Aspen, Colorado

One of the questions the author asked, was: What was the worst experience you have had in public with your reborn? I had to answer this one because my story was so absurd, and it could have happened to anyone, whether they had a real baby or a doll baby.

My husband and I were out shopping for the day, and as usual, I brought our reborn, Natalie, along. She goes everywhere with us, just as a real baby would. Because we are not trying to become a centerpiece of conversation, we use a car seat cover when we take her out with us. It stops a lot of the questions that would be difficult to answer without getting into a more prolonged conversation with random strangers.

The cover fits over the car seat completely and has Velcro at the front to keep it in place. This means that no one can see in when it is properly put together. We have been taking Nat around for so long now, that frankly, we forget most of the time that she is not just like every other baby. I think nothing of having her with us, and there is no awkwardness with the setup we have. We didn't get her to command the attention of others, we got her because we wanted a little girl to love.

So, we brought Nat into this restaurant, not a particularly upscale place, but not a bad place either. She was in her covered car seat, and the waitress came over to take our order. She asked us how old the baby was and we sort of mumbled a response. "2 months," was our usual answer.

"Awe. Can I see her?" she asked. I glanced at my husband, as we had been through this before. He smirked and let me handle it.

"She's sleeping right now," I told the waitress.

"I promise not to wake her up," she said. "I just want a little peek," she argued.

Who is this woman and why is she obsessed with my baby? I wanted to scream. I took a deep breath.

"She's very light sensitive," I told the waitress.

She then proceeded to tell me her life story, or rather that of the way her children, both girls and boys were at different stages of their lives. I humored her and listened. Eventually she decided to take our order.

I understand that some people might say, "If attention bothers you then why bring the doll?" I get that. But we are attached to her and treat her like family. My annoyance wasn't with someone being interested in our reborn, which would actually be understandable to some extent. My problem was that she didn't even know that we didn't have a real baby under that cover and she refused to let us alone. She was determined to see the baby. No one should hassle you if you say no to them seeing your kid, whether made of vinyl or not.

Just a few things for potential reborn parents to think about:

If you live in a small town, where you kinda know everyone, eventually people will have to realize that your kid never gets any bigger or any older. If you are still carrying the baby around in ten years in the same car seat, it is going to become rather obvious.

If you ever get pulled over by the cops with the baby in the car seat, it is going to be awkward. I would tell them it belongs to your daughter, granddaughter, whatever, but making a cop question your sanity when he pulls you over is not the best idea.

If you do have an odd moment where someone in public realizes your baby is a doll and asks questions, there are a number of routes you can go, depending on where you are at when it happens. I have told people that the reborn is a movie prop and we are searching for clothing for her...that can get messy if they want to know what movie...I have also told them I'm a photographer and she is a prop. Sometimes, I just smile and agree with them, feeling good that I have now entirely confused a nosy human being. Whatever you choose to do, own it. You have a right to be you.

Lena, 31

Seattle, Washington

I adopted my reborn girl, 3 pounds 12 ounces, named Daphne, in the fall of 2012. Since then, she has become my baby. I call her my baby, I take her out with me everywhere I can. She goes with me to go shopping, out with friends, etc. I've got a stroller for her, a baby carrier that I wear when we go to the park, she has a car seat and all of the other normal things one would find in a house with a baby.

Some people might think this is crazy, but for me, it works. I work from home. I live alone by choice. I am not interested in pursuing a relationship at this time, as I don't feel I'm ready for that yet. I want to figure out my career and what I want first. So, having a reborn works for me. I enjoy taking care of her, especially bathing, dressing and cuddling with her. I don't have to worry about a lot of the things other parents have to worry about, but then there are also some things I have to worry about that other parents don't.

One example of this is the strained relationship with my aunt that has come about since I adopted my reborn. My aunt and I have always been close, but she insists that caring for my doll is some sort of mental issue and I should stop doing it, as it is doing more harm to me than good. I really don't understand this, as I take care of her by choice. I call her my baby because I think of her that way. If you have ever held one of these ultra-realistic dolls, then you know what I mean. It is hard to think of them as anything other than a baby.

I have tried to explain to my aunt that I know the doll is a doll, and that this isn't a delusion, but she always has to mention it when we are together, reminding me that I am too old to play with dolls and that I should find a hobby. This is what she doesn't realize though. Taking care of my reborn, IS MY HOBBY. There are people who make dollhouses, people who paint or play an instrument, love their pets to the extreme. This is a hobby, too. I really don't see what the problem is.

She says that it is wrong to bring the doll out in public and let people think that it is a real baby. I don't get that either. I bring her out because I go out. I could not care less if anyone notices that I have her or not. I am not there to elicit a response from them. That's like saying you shouldn't ever walk your dog because some people might not like the breed. I do what I do because it makes ME happy.

I guess the divide will most likely continue between me and my aunt, unless she is willing to accept that I am devoted to my reborn and have no intentions of giving her up. I wouldn't ask her to stop quilting, because it makes her happy. Different strokes for different folks, or so the saying goes.

Christie and Will

Northern California

Will and I are in our late twenties, and unlike most of the couples we know personally, we have chosen not to have kids yet. We wanted to be sure we were ready for something with so much responsibility, so we've opted to wait until we feel that day has come.

I began reborning after being diagnosed with a disorder that prevents me from being able to stand for long periods of time. Prior to that I worked as a librarian, and Will works for a construction company in the area. I've always been into anything artsy and love doing crafty things that take a lot of time to create. I stumbled across a YouTube video of a woman making a reborn doll about a year and a half ago, and instantly thought it was something that I might have a real talent for.

Even though we have chosen not to have babies right now, I have always adored them. I can't resist oogling them when people bring their infants out in public, and I love all of the delicate folds of their skin and sleepy expressions on the faces of young babies. Being able to recreate those for others seemed like a job I would love to do.

Doing some research on reborn doll artists and how to begin creating the dolls, I discovered two things. First, this was not going to be a cheap venture. Secondly, I had a lot to learn. These dolls take weeks and in some cases, months to create. There are many steps between getting the kit and turning it into a fully reborned doll ready for adoption. At first, I was pretty intimidated by the idea of competing with some of the better artists out there.

I figured out quickly after beginning, that reborning isn't about competition anyway. Every artist has their own style and way of doing things, and each doll is a little different, even ones created by the same hand.

After getting into reborning and learning the ropes of heat set paints and the fine art and believe me, it is a fine art, of hand rooting hair, I found my calling. It might sound funny, but creating these dolls and customizing them to a client's request is somewhat like giving birth. It is a painfully slow and delicate process that requires a lot of time, attention to detail and dedication. I love my job now, and hope to be doing this for many years now.

Incidentally, even though we said we weren't ready for a child yet, we kept the first doll I completed, naming him Brendan. I take him with me to work every morning and as I sit in my studio crafting reborns for other people, I use him as my inspiration. I understand the fascination with this movement that people have. Holding a baby makes you feel good inside, and these guys are so real that you forget yourself while caring for them. Even my husband is guilty of falling in love with them, though I'm not sure he would admit it in writing for the purpose of inclusion in a book.

In my opinion, there have been a lot of fads that have passed by over the years, but these babies are here to stay. Don't believe me? Pick one up and hold one for a few minutes. You might find that you can't resist them either! Thank you for reading my story.

Author's note

Thanks so much for reading these reborn stories. This is volume one of a series, as it turned out that there are always more stories coming in, and in the interest of keeping this book relatively small, I will include more of the stories in the next volume. I hope that reading these stories has helped you to understand more about reborns and those who love them, or if you are already a reborn parent, that these stories have made you feel less alone and given you others that you can identify with.

What I found important about these stories, was the dedication and love that people are capable of showing to these babies. Perhaps people who would otherwise be terribly lonely, have found meaning and comfort in them. People who had no hobby before have grown into this and it has given them a sense of purpose. Artists that wanted to learn a new craft have been able to do so.

I guess the most important part of it all for me, is that everyone should be allowed to be who they are, without worry over what anyone else thinks. Other people are other people, and you are you. If the best version of yourself includes a reborn, then congratulations for finding something that makes you feel happy and complete. You will always encounter people who do not agree with your decisions, your way of life or something that you stand for, but it is no reason to change who you are. Be you, be happy.

Thank you for taking the time to read this book. I hope that you have enjoyed it and I would greatly appreciate a review anywhere you choose to leave one should you feel the book deserves one. I look forward to organizing the next book in this series.

As the art of reborning continues to advance, I'm sure there will be more and more people that become involved with it, both as adoptive parents and artists. In the next book I will include stories from people in other parts of the world involved with the reborn movement. Thanks again!

Made in the USA
Monee, IL
18 June 2021